TRAIN 01

The Collected Poems & Quotes

Dunns Diaite

Thank you
for being wonderful
people. Much love
to you and your
family.

Congrats on the
new baby

DOPEDUNNS™

This book took many years to create. It is proof that if you keep your mind and heart on your dreams and believe that they can come true, indeed with time they will manifest.

Always stay positive

Always keep imagining

Always keep creating

Your own reality

For in the universe of abundance

Anything is possible

Table of Contents

The Winds of Life

Mother of the Motherless

Into the center is a jezebel

Of sweet proportions

With beautiful smile

Of a devil's grin.

She favors among her children,

Negligible towards most.

Her balance is slanted one sided

Based on how it's viewed

But she cares not,

Simply walks in a fast pace

With her children

Scattering behind to follow on

A treadmill road to anywhere

And nowhere.

Mother of the motherless children,

She is life.

Sunrise

The moon cascaded

In a cloud of misty rain.

Still as the silent

Screams of street lights

That shines on the corner

Of history filled pavements.

Cold air gives deep

Massages to my bones

As I turtle into a hoodie

Cotton filled as slave fields.

I embrace its origin n

Feel warmth of the sun

That bled my Ancestors' backs.

Sitting on my stoop

Awaiting on sunrise

To take my soul to heaven.

Lonely Nights

When everyone sleeps

I'm awake with the demons

Who shed light to dark sides

Only dreamt of by prophets.

As truth is twisted

In vortex of reason,

I steer pass the ghostly deed

Who feeds off giving fear.

Unable to grasp my soul

For I am one with the night

Moon of the Saharan desert,

Forever lost in the dust of God.

Full Circle

Never would of thought years later

I would be

At the bus station staring

From the other side of the road

Motionlessly daydreaming

About me looking

Toward the bus stop, saying

I will never be in that scene

Funny how life goes full circle.

Money Isn't Everything

Dig deeper n you'll find peace

Bigger than da big dipper!

Cuz money ain't got no soul,

Money ain't got no heart

You can have all the money

In the world

You'll still be right

Where ya start.

The Heart Speaks

We strive to find purpose

And stress everything in between

Happiness is hard to achieve

If desires of the world

Are not at arm's reach.

Distorted hopes of "could be's"

Get you out of sync

With the real "what it is", and

You end up missing out

On the beauty of your life!

It is not what's in your head

But what's in front of your heart

That matters the most.

Bless

Never stress unexpected turns

If anything,

They make things more interesting

Pain, drama, heartache, struggles

Are all there

To make your life more zestful

So if you have a crazy day, smile

Because your life isn't boring.

Highway to Destiny

Life is a highway

And we are the cars on it

Whenever we stop or break down

The traffic keeps on going,

So down shift your clutch and

Give it all the gas you got

Enjoy the wind against your hood,

And the dust

Behind your rear bumper

Because one day you have to get out

And take an exit.

Goodbye NYC

Old days turn to new

As new friends turn to old

Alchemist of love turns

Ghetto to gold

Soaring the dirt filled hole

Digging for sunlight

As empire of the city

Shines and leaves

Sadness on the road I-95.

Highways to home

Is never just one exit

My heart becomes strong and weak

At the same time as wheels spin,

In the rearview mirror

is the image of the

New York skyline

Till next time,

Train of Thought

I'm ghost in my own mind.

Prosperity

There is a power in goodness

While the first thing learned

Is hardest to forget

The last thing learned

Is as hard to let go as the first,

Staying in peace

Will lead to prosperity

It is easy to do wrong

& doing the right thing is hard

But every paradise has its price

And everything good

Is worth the life.

Doubt Lives

Figment imagination of smiles

Turns to frowns of fury

Heavy heart

From the weight of surroundings

Bare back so it stings

Much more while

Strength sits on paths of lost

Emotions and self questioning!

No answer to the problems

Formulating as the clock ticks

Time watches of a decaying soul

In front of the condors

Bird of life spreads its wings

Only to wrap around my neck

To feast on confidence of

Unpromising futures.

Strength Within

The monk sidewinders in the shadows

Of the eagle's fist

The dragon dances

In the lake of darkness

His eyes bright

As the moon's reflection

On the still water

Steamy breaths as he twirls

Motionless with heart heavy,

The beaded covered monk in

Meditating posture

Opens his eyes

As the dragon fades into a mist

Monk breathes in fear sweating

Knowing the dragon

Is a reflection of his inner danger.

Simplicity

I sometimes catch myself

Lying to my soul

Because desire has a way of

Manipulating my true vision

To see exactly what is real and

What is a lust,

Altering my beliefs for

The benefit of wanting

Evolving into needing

Therefore must have.

Simplicity is the road to

Salvation from

One's desire.

Humbleness

As bad as

your day, week, or month is

Always remember that

There is someone else in the world

Who would die to have

Your so called bad day,

For them it would be paradise.

The things we stress

In life the most,

We fail to realize their true

Unimportance in reality.

If you can't take it to the grave

Then don't stress it

Life is a balance of good and bad

When bad swings around,

Still embrace it and keep living.

DColors

I am not black

Not African, not American raised

Not Muslim, not hood,

Not a college graduate

Not dark, not any of these things

I am something much more

I am human first!

Show love

As much as we try to find

Differences between each other

We must realize we are all one.

One species, one kind, one blood.

ONE LOVE.

Peace.

Fear

Fear is the inability

To understand something

Outside of our own

Comprehensive elements.

It is the abundance of realizing

One is capable

Of being in line of termination

Or that one

Is not in control of the situation,

That awakes the

Feeling of helplessness

This matures into what we know

As fear.

It is a natural element

we can learn

To suppress but not erase.

The Past

Set point on the sunrise

I point east and bow

To the mountains

Behind my shadow I leave tracks

On the sand my ancestors slumbered

The mother of the nature

I seek to be in tune

As my lungs occupy

The winds which sing

Folk tales of the past

The trees dance and

The eagle glances

My destination is within

The center of my universe

I wander forth towards my true self

Waiting on the day to see Africa.

Nickel Bag

My nickel brown bag of funk

Got me tired but woke up my soul

I travel in the life stream

Where the angel awaits

To touch my every essence

Essentially

Locking my heart

In a flower of roses,

The thorns flow from my stem

To blossom her field

As the skyline glows brighter

Than full moon on a Brooklyn sky.

The War

The serpent flows beneath the water

I rest in the fountain

Valley of springs

Dove elongates its arms

As deep as the sea

Truth lies between vision of the

Bird and the prey

Struggle for survival

Rest in a fate

Uncontrolled notion of greatness.

The bird dives,

I the water cannot escape their war

Inside me they struggle.

The dove eats the serpent

As I realize my innocence has

killed by my hatred.

Power

Power is a neutral element

Adapted for a positive solution

Or negative destruction,

It is powerless

Until mixed with the will

Of another which brings it meaning.

This is true to religion, behavior,

Science, thought, and life.

Self power is only gained

When this is understood and adapted

Through your everyday living.

Metro Area

The night sky glistens

In dark bliss

Train screams,

Inside passengers aboard on

The final section

Of their journeys.

Hardness fills the air

As lights shine

Surrounding brick buildings

Tick tock onward on tracks,

Blue pigs with hats

Tricks who trick a dollar

Out of your pocket traps

Through it all I find peace

In a concrete jungle

Where the lion muffle

Melodies of reggae in my ear,

Train of Thought

It is definitely

A NYC moment.

Full Continue

Each n every person has their own

Personal dream or goal

All will struggle reaching that

Sense of completion,

Yet when we reach

That dream or goal

We realize there are more

Repressed goals

Ready to be conquered.

LIFE IS A CIRCLE;

I HOPE IT LOOPS

AROUND TWICE.

Rules of the Game

1) Life is never guaranteed no matter how much you plan.

2) Lead, do not follow.

3) Stress is part of the game. If you scratch on an 8 ball pocket, you have to rack it up and keep playing.

4) As long as you are alive you have not failed anything, because it can be accomplished tomorrow.

5) Be humble to yourself and others.

The Air I Breath

I can feel it in the air

How we all have different emotions

We try to exhaust through words

Feelings turn to written lines

Canned into a paragraph

Of our mind with the cover

Our book being our faces,

I feel the pain,

Happiness, creativity

Flowing in the air.

Keep writing.

Brooklyn

A star shines in the Brooklyn sky

Glittering over people

Who lay Bed in the Stuy

I stare at the light

Thinking how could it be

That though covered in darkness,

The star I can see.

Star smiles and whispers

"Little boy don't cry,

Only when you fall

Do wings spread and fly high",

With this I lay my head

And say good night

To a star that shines

In the Brooklyn sky.

Adversity

The notion to fight fears

Is better than avoiding them,

Running away prolongs the situation

Intensifies the fears greater than

If they were faced

From the beginning,

Facing fears,

Even if faced and lost

Is always a win.

Acceptance

Accepting the fact

That no one owes you anything

Is understanding that

You owe yourself everything,

Learn and appreciate

Your unique worth,

Life is Good.

A Book

The open book of creation is held

In the hands of one's perspective

The freedom of joy is the balance

Contained within everyone's heart,

The pages,

Nothing more than documentation

Of one's journey

A piece of memory

Forever lost in library of time.

We shall all close

The last page of our book of life

So we should try to make it

A damn good read,

- enjoy your life.

Modern Beasts

Beasts with the nature of sheep

Rise only in the truth

Called by serpents!

Ignorance blinds those

Who see not but only reality,

Lost in complex of simplicity.

Ghosting

Every time I write my soul cries

Words can't express

How my soul flies

Wana let it out, so I

Turn verbs to a passion

Collectively order paragraphs

To emotion

Zone out,

speaking folk tales till I'm open

Raw like concrete,

The hard blocks of Brooklyn

Poetry in motion

Deep like the ocean for

When I write I be Ghosting.

Man who Flew

Man who can fly as eagles

Is never grounded

To the belief of the masses

His heart a visionary

Telescope of stars that

See the blindness of others.

His mind a philosopher of

Prophetic scriptures

Shines a torch of hope

His hands share wealth

Before he consumes for himself

His feet tower mountain peaks

Overlooking the skyline of life

His simplicity is a complex

Gesture of old wisdom

His knowledge vast

Yet empty for new beginnings

Train of Thought

Artistic as the sunrise

And the falling rain!

The man who flies as eagles

Spends his best times with crows

Equality is his soul for he knows

The sky belongs to no one and all.

Stay True

The Key

The key to the door

I was raised on sum other shit

Different than the life

You're used to,

See I'm trapped

Between the lines of two worlds

A constant struggle to figure out

Who I am and what I stand for

Questions I ask myself dig deeper

To ancestral pain

Embracing future Happiness

And every day is a new chapter,

Looking for the key to the door.

Inner Passion

It's more like,

Live to find out

Or die to never know

No time to waste

On past or even the present

Show me the next page

To the book you call living,

And I'll show you everything

You need to know about yourself

If and only if,

You can handle

The reality of what I am.

Twisted

Fact or fiction?

The fact of the matter

Is that fact is fiction

If the fact is revealed

in a fictional circumstance.

Yet still being a fact,

Makes the reality of fiction

Possible

To make fact real

But still fiction.

Therefore fact is real and fiction

At the same time.

Fact is fiction and

Fiction is fact.

New Beginning

I sit in the same seat

As I once did 3 years ago

Looking across the water

At a dream and realizing

I'm back to the beginning,

But this is a new person

With a much more open mind

And understanding of life,

I am ready!

Insanity

Losing the absence of actuality

Is the same as being dead!

Grasping reality

Seems to only be real

In a delusion state

Contributing to factors

Of confusion

While the mind plays tricks

In order to keep

A bent balance of an already

Unbalance state of mind.

Therefore what it may seem

Is far from what it is,

In actuality the only absence

Is your sanity,

Insanity.

Liars

The concept of a pathological liar

Is simple as it is complex.

It is not that one believes

In the lies told,

But more of a complex

Pyramid of lies

To support the main lie.

The top of the pyramid

Is the main lie & the bases are

Peripheral lies constructed to

Support the main lie.

Each is very thought out

As even the main lie can become

A base lie to support

Another now on top.

It is a revolving triangle of

Deception.

Destiny

All we can do is try,

If destiny wants

Us to change the world

Then it will happen.

If not at least

We've changed ourselves,

So it is a good start and

Not a bad ending

If it does not work out.

A Hand in Hand

Which is bigger?

The vast universe or

The vast potential of a human brain

We currently explore

Less than 5 percent of both.

Is it possible they play an

Interactive role?

It all plays back to

"answers of life are within us"

Meaning figure out

Our brain's full power

And we solve the universe.

Sounds crazy right?

Just something to sleep on.

Wisdom of the Old Man

Wisdom is a factor of time,

It cannot be bought

Only attained

Through age and knowledge,

Wisdom is a factor of power

It can be as unlimited and vast

As the universe,

True wisdom is self attained

Through experience

With an open mind.

Not Fair

Have you ever wanted to live

Your life a certain way?

So much that it kills you

On the inside?

Makes you wonder

Why destiny and desire

At times never walk hand in hand

Or in some cases,

Don't walk at all.

Give It to You

Moses wrote on stone tablets

Because he thought

It was unbreakable,

Martin took us to the mountain top

Thinking we would see the light,

Gandhi starved himself

Of worldly possessions

Hoping we would

Embrace the humbleness.

I speak about things I see to open

The eyes of all my people

Regardless of my ending,

My reason is everlasting

At its beginning.

Love is strong

People really want to have

Something to believe in,

Prophet not an object to the devil

I tell truth even when

I speak lies,

Smile at tears with no fear to die

No fear of any man

No care for any brand

Only God,

Good enough reason to believe.

Circles

Same shit dif day

Life is a circle

Just like the globe

So fuck it

If my state of mind got me thinking

It's a triangle or any other

Mathematical shape

I can think of,

Just means I see life

In another perspective

It's still part of the same circle,

That's all.

A Dream

I want to be

A part of something more

And I'll die

A sad man if I never accomplish it

So please understand

Why I am living for a dream

And why I sacrifice

Everything I got

Just to grasp it.

Senegal

There is more to me

Than what meets the eye,

The smile, or the person.

I am the untold history of

My grandmothers

The African sand

Soul of the Black man

In his true essence

I am greatness.

Green Grass

Have you ever strived for something

Because you think it's so great,

When you get there

You feel the same

As you did

Before you strived for it?

The grass is not greener

On the other side

It is just because

You looked so hard

At the grass you are on

That you only see dirt

Missing the beautiful grass

And flowers on top.

Finding Peace

Peace of mind doesn't seem to win

When everything is going wrong

I pray for those who lost

Their peace of mind

At the same time

I'm going insane because

I myself need prayer

For I cannot find

My peace.

The Hurdles

A person is not simply judged on

What they have accomplished

But by overcoming the obstacles

They faced

In order to become successful,

You ARE your own obstacles

Failure is only if you

Believe in it.

Peace God.

I just want to enjoy my time

Till I return

In the meanwhile

I will smile for the lost ones

Try to maintain

For life is a constant

Balance to normal

While normality

Is slowly turning insane,

All I can do is stay true

So please save me

From the evil that men do.

What It Is

Ghostly dreams of day mares

Consist on constant confusion

The mental capacity of illusions

Trade for the soul

Far valuable than less

What you strive for may not equate

To the power of your death.

Who dictates what is living?

And who replied what is not?

Are we free or bound

In the thought process

Of those who never think?

Or are we just

In the motion of time

To be phased out

On history's capacity?

Every war is factor

Train of Thought

To the future

Do u remember every single soul

That died

To make your present?

Or is it only relevant

To the victors?

Recognition of deep connection

Swims in shallow waters

The life vest of love

Knows no discrimination

Only the limited weight

Of what his heart

Can bear to stay afloat.

The key to her essence

Dances in the glittering

Reflection of the lover's eyes

As kisses are gift wrapped

As the key of doors

A simple touch grasps stars

Her smile time lapsed in his memory

Train of Thought

Forever repeating.

First element of love

Tends to last the longest

For first loves are never

Meant to be forgotten!

Through love we learn,

In learning we live,

In living we love.

Life is a cycle, Bless.

So Simple

Can it be

That it was all so simple?

The concept of living

Has been altered by dead men

Yet their visions

Still exist past their existence.

Confusion,

chaotic views, ignorance,

Hate, selfishness, materialism,

Need for success, careers,

Can it be that

It was all so simple?

And through time,

We have become the slaves

Of our desires?

Lessons

I see life through many eyes

Vivid thoughts of bugged out

Cycles of lost souls

Who dwell in forbidden crossroads.

Of truth come lies

Accompanied by one's opinion

The lesson, simple in equation

Becomes the calculus of deviation.

The Road

Life's blessing and happiness

Is a state of mind.

You are the life you live,

If you're not happy with yours,

Change it.

It all starts

By thinking positive and

Not loving things that really

Have no value.

Follow the road to your destiny

With a calm mind and open heart.

Sin

If God knows all you do

Before you do it when you sin,

Is it because God

Set you up to fail?

If it was written that

You are going to sin,

Is the sin wrong?

Or is it right

That the sin happens,

Since it is going

According to plan?

Advise

Life is too short to worry

About all the small things that

Make you not enjoy it.

Whatever it is

That makes you happy,

Do it.

You only get one chance,

One shot, one time, one life.

Live it with a smile on your face.

Mountains of Hardship

Wealth

Wealthy is only in the concept

Of what you find most at value

Rich in life can mean

More than just money

Rich in health,

Rich in love,

Rich in happiness!

You are only poor if

Your definition of rich is limited

To manmade means of transaction,

When there are millions of things

To be rich in for free.

Dwelling Dreams

Is it worth it?

Days turn to night

Daydreams to nightmares

Of mental anguish

Insomniac to the realization that

What I'm pushing for

Is not worth the strength put in

Give it all for the world in return

Leave nothing for myself

What's the point of it all

If I live,

For the benefit of everyone else?

Planetary Love Lust

Play station of hearts

Can't be won in a game

Switch lane n cruise parallel 360

To be x-boxed as past love.

Breath of fresh air

To your mars roses

Thorns move too swift to get caught

In a spider's web

As love lost turns to black holes

An open milky way of pain forever

Drank by sorrow.

Broken Heart

Love is dumb empty

Like the parking lot,

So never

Give your heart enough

For them to find

A parking spot.

Math It Up

Infinity of Omega is Theta.

Infinity of the end is death.

Tell me we don't use math

Beyond numbers

And I reply your conclusion

To life's formula is false.

Breaking Point

I tried so hard to live

Outside of myself

That now I have

Completely lost myself

Just walking on a road to nowhere

Kicking up dust,

Daydreaming

About nothing and everything

Being able to think is much more

Of a curse than a blessing

Speaking quotes too deep for some

To understand,

I know they faking like they do but

I walk this road alone

Destination is unknown as I wonder

If happiness will ever

Cross my path.

Trapped in my own mind

I'm stuck in this life forever

The more I want this to change,

The more it seems to stay the same

Full circle of the same problems

I think disappear

Boomerang back to the start.

World spins, time ticks,

Locations change but still living

The same shit in different days

Claustrophobic to my own self

With no help of getting out.

I'm stuck in this life

Forever with no doubt.

Manhood

The warriors of virtue

Battle with the boogieman

Who stands hand in hand,

The heart in one,

The mind in another.

Boogieman grins for he knows

His defensive stance

Is the illusion of man.

He lives

Through hearts and minds fueled

By desire and sins, 666...

The 3 moons of death

Give power to 18 black angels.

So when you turn 18

Is when you're visible to him.

Coming of age heading to hell

Without ever knowing.

The Future

Death is an exhausted strength

That doesn't rejuvenate.

Families of different faces

In uniform

As all their hearts

Beat aches of sadness

That flow through their eyes

As they watch

A piece of themselves drop

6 feet beyond grasp

Forever.

Concept of Illusion

The night ghost

Haunting me in my deep thoughts

With eyes that see truth beyond the

Shade of the light.

The darkness is my sanity

Yet the ghost is my fear.

In the mirror where he lies,

He whispers.

"Come into the light"

I smile back and whisper

"My dark skin is perfect

Just the way it is".

Tears of pain

Dreams are meant to fly mid-range

To the clouds of despair and die

As disappointment gathered in

Bundles that rain drops of

"What ifs" which turns

To "would not's"

By the time it hits the ground.

I lay there motionless

On the rainy day

And feel my soul elevate

Then gravitate downward

In a raindrop.

Tears fall but they blend

With the disappointed dreams

That came from the heavens.

Devils

The devil sent 666,

So u can rest 6 feet deep

By 6 feet long

And 6 degrees earth.

Today you got to break away

From all the hecticness

Of our misconstructed reality.

Today you get to breathe easy and

Let your eyes relax.

Today you are free

As the caged bird

Released so rest in peace.

I'll miss you,

And for a second my heart stopped

To thinking

About the last time I saw you.

Life is too short.

The Voyager

You just can't

Understand the emotions

Running through my vain

As I reminisce on

My past life of Africa

The feeling of paradise I lived.

As I sit in the darkness I realize

I will never be complete,

What I was, died a long while ago

With time.

My peace of mind forever twisted

In my mind

Until the day I rest in peace,

Damn.

Nature

There's a butterfly

Caught in a spider's web.

If you save the butterfly

The spider dies.

If you help the spider

The butterfly dies.

How do you save them both?

Nike it

If you hope high

At times dreams crash down harder

Yet in order for dreams

To come true

You need high hopes.

Ironic isn't it

Life is what is it,

JUST LIVE IT.

World Watches

At times

We have a privilege of

Denying reality

The things we stress

Are nothing compared to

Those who fight to simply

Push back death.

Palaces of slums

Where food is a desired dream

And humanity is rejected.

The world is dying

And we

Still have yet to wake up.

Love Blossoms

Sleepless Lust

Life is but a dream,

What does it take to wake up?

When I do open my eyes,

Where will it be that I slumber?

Is it deeper than

My mind can wonder?

Or can I travel to its distance

Beyond the yonder.

Tylenol PM me to a place I wana see

And a man I am to be

To the heavens so above

N a girl I'll forever love.

Love is Blind

The blind woman

Opened my eyes to dimensional

Views deeper than the tears

I see fall

For she feels first and

Sees second.

More in tune than my signals

Are able to elaborate

In the midst of conversation and

Old school blues tunes

The sadness lifts up and my heart

Smiles.

Enter Fall

Summer day

U make my temperature rise as your

Rays hug my skin

So warmly that it melts my soul.

You give desire to

Green filled pastures

As autumn infects color unto leaves

To bring life to silent landscapes.

As the wind blows gently

Singing melodies,

The fallen pieces of the big tree

Ballet

In perfect harmony on the ground,

Won't you be around

A little much longer?

A Woman

A girl worth wandering

The oceans for is love

That uplifts you

Wondering the keys to her spirit.

Girls are deeper than

Skin tones or body structures,

Analyze and realize

So you can appreciate

The good things about women

Not just what they

Chose to show you or you see

On the exterior

Women are the key

To all of your existence

Honor them

As the Goddesses they truly are.

Sade Poem

No ordinary love

As I paradise your sweetest taboo

I cherish the day you give

Me your kiss of life,

Jezebel you took my heart n

Crowned me the king of sorrow, yet

Still I stand by your side

For your love is king

Love is stronger than pride

As I fall deep

Infatuated by your melody

Of being a smooth operator.

Support System

I find peace in people and places

I normally would not expect

Humbleness dangles at the key

On the door to self salvation

Behind the door are the people

Who hold chains linked

To your back with hooks

Manufactured by love

Your support system.

For whenever you fall,

The chains extend

Holding you upright.

They smile as they whisper

"We got you fam, if you drop

we all Fall".

Cycle

Distorted views of love

Are far from conceptual reality

The heart speaks in tongues

Unaware that

The mind is comprehensively lost

Within the views of emotion.

Yet the notion of the red rose

Blossoms

Bright as the lip stick worn

For a heart scorned is nothing more

Than a broken stem

That seeds a weed

In the garden of love.

Loving is to enslave one's desire

In the acceptance of another

As the cycle plays both ways.

Good Times

I feel good...

I'm right with God

Right with moms

Right with my African past n

Right with my unwritten future.

Most of all right with myself,

Enjoying my life, by any means.

Self Worth

Feeling good today.

Happiness isn't found anywhere

It doesn't exist anywhere

But inside of yourself.

Love everything about yourself

Unconditionally

And you will always

Find the light

In this dark world.

One Day

She, lost in the curls

Of rooted afros

Held by genuine ignorance of

Simplicity

Is an angel in the land of bitches.

She questions not what is

But defines it through

Joyous experiences of life itself

And all without losing

Her sense of pride

As a true woman.

Love Comes and Goes

They say love comes and goes

But it is us who

Temporarily leave it.

Connections can span through past

The grasp of time

Space and dimensions.

For the space attained

In the heart powers

Lost ones revived as if

Yesterday is present

And reminiscent emotions

Complete full circle.

You see--love comes,

we go and always return to it.

For any life without

love isn't truly living.

One love.

The Break Up

For your love is two deep,

Too sweet to jump into

With just a leap.

You see me in ways

I wish to see myself,

Staying in that part of love

Keeping in good health.

I see others but

They don't understand,

A unique one as myself

I am not an ordinary man.

You wish and dream of love

That once was to be,

You say I don't know

But yet it's meaningful to me.

The wonderful is worth waiting for,

For that day isn't far

Train of Thought

When I come knocking on that door.

My mind is true

But my heart is stubborn,

For I say love is

The warmth being burned.

You speak I listen

But hear what I'm missing.

In between the words and verbs

Interacting, kissing.

Complication is the heart while

Love is the game

We all play for different reasons,

Why two loves aren't ever the same.

Streets Are Watching

Praying on Daydreams

I ain't on da dean I'm on the lean.

Should pray n do the right shit,

Lost in da dark

Cuz my demons doing nightshifts.

Overtime, chasing good times

N bugged nights,

Aiming for bright lights.

Only to realize,

I'ont like this who am I.

Can't go back;

Feel trapped but scared to die.

What's da point of question

If da answer is better lied?

Question my point of living,

If soul is better died.

Déjà Vu

Back in the field of dreams

Where things fall back

To how they used to seem

Quiet nights and dropped Hondas

Rolling by

Staring at stars as time flies

Same place, same faces

With new attitude

Fast forward from a kid

To a man with cool blues

Loving the vibe of my city

Nothing to do but somehow

I stay busy,

Life's a dream.

In God We Trust

In God we trust

Behind the judge who's actions

Are nothing but,

Power given to man by ancestors

To control man himself

If they can control your life

With rules

They control your soul

It is not about good or bad,

It is about power

Fuck the judge,

I only have one

And that's God.

Blending Complex

When you try too hard

To fit in a game,

You get played.

When you try too much of the same,

You get slayed.

When you try too little,

It stays the same.

So you have to stay neutral

In this game to change.

Cat Woman

Lie down, open up.

Put ya soul out da door

Let judgment rest outside

Because in this room

It's about money

Cash for gold where fortune is sold

In a double lipped hole of hoes

Zombies roam nights

In search for paradise,

Time flies the soul dies

A happiness of sad trick for trix.

Ass out, nut for bucks.

Pretty lady,

Don't sell yourself

For devil's games

Where death is certain

But life is not.

Da Pusher

Birds of a feather

Don't flock together,

In the sky where clouds

Are crack houses n

The sun is a sailing lighthouse of

Project buildings.

These birds fly together only

To clip each other's wings

With bullets at the

Horizon of death.

Their feathers and hearts

Shaded of crows

As they hang on pole lines waiting

On their next prey,

Flying their altitude

Only means crashing down

Cuz shiesty dealers are birds.

Share

Most spend thousands of dollars

In college

And still come out confused.

Civilized but are we really civil?

As we watch others

Sleep on the streets

Ignore what our eyes see,

Forget the bad days

Our lives are constructed

To focus only on self.

A man alone cannot change the world

For the better

If the only interest

Is for himself.

Street Life

Understanding

The state of mind elevation

Is beyond the

Grasp of your reality.

The twilight zone of the road

Is constructed

Between the black and white bricks

Of saturated stars

In the multiversity known

As hood life.

NO Guns, Only Old School

WEAPONS DESTROY LIVES,

When you knuckle up you win,

Even when you lose.

To live yet another day

Of challenges

That will arise.

Mountain Top

Life is but a dream,

Yet the future is taken

In its present.

Slumber in thoughts

On hope filled nights

Shines guidance like

The North Star.

What am I but a peasant

Born to be king,

Who rests in

The arms of the dragon.

Torched is my heart on the journey

Pain is a small price to pay

For a wake up in Greatness.

Filter

Through the smoke screens of

People's bullshit,

I see the truth is

Darker and lonelier

Than I could ever have anticipated

In the land of real recognize real

Rest many fakers,

So every once in a while u gots

To filter out your circles.

Art Who Goes There

A man's worst enemy is Fear

For nothing is given

Without it being earned

At some point in time

Go hard for yours,

Fear will never match up

To the love of your art.

Death

Death is not simply

A physical aspect

One can perish

While still being alive

The disconnect from one self

In search for exterior gain

Has the capability of

Subconscious mental destruction,

The need to BE in this world,

At times

Causes one to

Unconsciously self neglect

The true needs of their soul

Proving the struggles

To live itself

Is cased with death,

If one fails

To stay true to

Themselves.

Chasing the Cool

The bold truth

Slumbers in dark clouds,

Emitting rain of tears.

What we know is only

A portion of that we see,

Yet looking at the picture

Abstract in its form

Shows not

The figure of the painter.

Life doesn't get anything

But more confusing

N the closer you come

To being perfect

Is when you've lost track

Of it all.

You see a bird flying free;

I only see that it falls.

Train of Thought

The gravity of people's pressures

Is enough to give back in its all,

A simple man

Trapped in a maze to belong.

Only fit in between

Where everything is just wrong.

Let It BE

To see beyond your grasps

Is not attainable,

You believe in destiny yet try hard

To control that which you cannot.

Your desires are wrapped

In a gift box of fears,

And are headed

To a future of reminiscing tears

Created by your own hands.

Destiny, the formula

Of everything and nothing

Steers only in one direction,

Even if one travels

In the wrong lane,

Against the traffic of

So called normality.

Simplicity

Life's Lemons

Death is the one thing

That joins any and

All of us together.

Why does it always take

The death of someone you know

To realize

That there is more to life

Than the things we stress about.

TIME IS TICKING,

LIFE IS FOR THE LIVING.

DEATH IS FOR THE NEXT,

ENJOY THE AIR YOU ARE GIVEN.

Do what makes u happy.

You only get one life, so one love.

Reality

At times we spend so long

Looking out the box,

That we lose a grasp

Of what is reality.

Lucky Who?

Successes and failures

Have resulted from

Your own actions,

Not chance or luck.

Dream Chaser

The one who ignores

What remains constant,

Is constantly chasing

Everything that is not.

Neglectful Power

Position of status

Does not justify

The actions

Of criminality.

Resilience

Even eyes in

The shadows

Shine bright

In the light.

So Simple yet So Neglected

It really doesn't matter

At the end of the day.

All you have is your life.

It is the only thing you truly own.

Too Good?

Being good at everything

Is equal to being bad

At everything.

In the end you are left

At a standstill

With a gridlock determination

As Jack of all trades

Is a master to none.

BE Patient

Sometimes trying too hard

To get something

Might change your destiny of

Receiving it in the first place.

Who Writes The Rules?

Laws of man

Created by man

Are only for the benefit

Of man's greed and need of status.

Live

A person dies

When they no longer want to live,

Just because you are alive

Does not mean you are truly living.

A Mind Set

One Love

One God

One Earth

One Species

Different perspectives.

Science

Reflection of the internal

Is the true characteristic

Of being a Human,

Knowing oneself.

Normality

A normal life is only in the eyes

Of the person living it.

Everything outside of

Him or herself

Is abnormal until interfaced

And accepted

With one's own life.

Light in the Darkness

Losing someone or something

Valuable to you

Is the biggest empowerment

In a destructive situation.

Careful What You Learn

Hatred is born from fear,

Fear is the mother of

Things we do not understand.

Hatred is not understanding

Therefore rejecting

What you don't understand

As fear.

Create

Life

Is what you make of it,

Bottom line.

Values

Money

Is everything

In the world

And nothing

In the world of love.

Faith

Believe

In Truth and Love.

Reason does not allow you to

Yet Faith always does.

Breathe Easy

Don't worry

About the present

My brother,

The future is GREAT

Healer

Suffering can only

Be cured by medicine,

Patience,

Or love.

Shop for Ur Soul

Material objects

Got the world

Crooked and bent

Out of shape.

Spread Knowledge

Wisdom has no purpose

If it is retained

Only within one individual.

Don't Change

Natural beauty

Is better,

In any form

Of expression.

Death Of

Values of morality

Only reach full efficiency

When one accepts mortality

While still living.

Hidden in the rear

To not have loved

Is to walk

Without looking behind

At least once

To days where the heart

Was the ruler of time.

Love Urself

Even a hawk

Is an eagle among crows,

And a crow an eagle

Amongst pigeons.

Truth is Buried

Why is it

That the dead man

Is always right?

Try Sum New

Staying in the normality

Of one's comfort zone

Sometimes blinds our perspective

On everything around us.

Step out, live life.

Peace

Devils Tunes

As long as money

Plays a factor in music

Or in any form of Art

Including life itself

It is forever tainted.

Reminisce

Reminiscing about the past

Does not change the present

Look forward and keep pushing.

Mornings

```
Every morning

I wake up and think

"Today is the first day

of the rest of my life"

And you know what,

It feels pretty great.
```

Da Government

```
SAME PREDATOR

New faces

Same prey.
```

Devolve

Human evolution;

Wider freeways,

But narrower viewpoints.

True Blood

Never deny

Your true nature

Feed your soul.

Scale

Always take the time

To take a pause and

Stick back to the basics.

Normal

The True definition of normality

Is that everything is abnormal.

It is the acceptance of

Abnormal things

That manifest them to what we call

Normal.

Life is a Drink

Same Kool-Aid

Of sunrises and sunsets

Different cups

Of experiences.

The Basics

No matter how many people

I can strive or try to be.

My Heart lets me know who

I really am at the end of the day.

Plan

Live life to the fullest

As if to die tomorrow

And plan ahead

As if to live forever.

Purpose

What is the point

Of wishing

If everything I desire

Is bad for me?

Real Talk

Thinking too much

Is the same thing

As not doing shit,

Cuz u ain't doing shit

But thinking too much.

Truth

We take a lot of things

For granted you and I,

Granted we only give a little.

Yin

Every cause has an effect,

Nothing just all of a sudden

Happens without reason.

Yang

Just gave a homeless guy 5 bucks,

And somehow my walk home

Did not seem as cold when

I realized he has nowhere

To walk to except the coldness

Of people's hearts.

Conclusion of New

I am the hope

That destroys dreams

To embrace nightmares

Of joy and despair.

Who's Fooling Who?

When you try

To fool everyone,

You only end up

Fooling yourself

In the end.

Desire

I realize

The only person

Holding me back

From getting what I want

Is me.

Flowers Born in Bricks

Fairness does not exist

In the concrete jungle.

Barely faint signs

Of joy and gross pain in bundles.

Myth of Perfection

Practice doesn't make perfect,

Because once you reach perfection,

You still desire to practice

For constant perfection

Is an illusion.

Mind Games

I/E (I over E)

Equals getting through

The cloudiness of

People's Bullshit.

Intellect over Emotion

Is at times

The safest method

In the Mind Games.

?uestion

HOW COME THE MOST WISE

AMONGST MEN LIVE NOT LONG LIVES

YET ARE MORE WISE IN MESSAGE

THAN THOSE OF OLD AGE?

The Push

No matter how much

Someone is faithful,

If there is no will behind it.

Then it means nothing.

Da Man

A man who is not afraid

To die for what he believes in,

Can never be defeated.

If he is tricked

Into believing something

He is long defeated

Before he even starts.

Price 4 Ur Life

```
EVERYBODY'S

GOT A PRICE,

SO WHAT DOES

YOUR LIFE COST?
```

Talk is Cheap

THINGS ARE EASIER

SAID THAN DONE,

AND SAID

IS ALWAYS DONE.

Overcome

If pain is life,

And life is worth dying for.

How much pain

Are you willing to take,

For a chance to really live?

Dusting your courage

Trying to learn

How to face

Failures and rejection.

Love

I love life,

So I

Stay positive

For any day

Can be my last.

Wisdom

A man who begins

To somewhat understand,

First learns only

That he knows nothing.

Day

Every day is a lesson learned.

Does not matter

If it was a good day or not,

I still learned my lesson.

Born Perfect

Perfection is attained

When you are born,

Searching for it elsewhere

Is simply a successful

Attempt at confusion.

I Am

Speaking with the knowledge

That my ancestors gave

Knowledge of the truth

Is in the answer of slaves.

Beauty

Attractions are

Nothing more than distractions.

What we measure as complete success

In reality to the universe

Is merely a fraction.

FREEDOM IS EVERYTHING.

Made in the USA
Columbia, SC
02 December 2019

84217450R00107